Horace H. Houghton

A System of Philosophy

The order of mind, as governing matter, in the construction and progress of all things in nature, and particularly applied in the construction and advancement of man

Horace H. Houghton

A System of Philosophy
The order of mind, as governing matter, in the construction and progress of all things in nature, and particularly applied in the construction and advancement of man

ISBN/EAN: 9783337239626

Printed in Europe, USA, Canada, Australia, Japan

Cover: Foto ©Thomas Meinert / pixelio.de

A SYSTEM OF PHILOSOPHY.

THE

ORDER OF MIND,

AS

GOVERNING MATTER,

IN THE

CONSTRUCTION AND PROGRESS

OF

ALL THINGS IN NATURE,

AND

PARTICULARLY APPLIED

IN THE

CONSTRUCTION AND ADVANCEMENT

OF

MAN.

CHICAGO:
GUILBERT & CLISSOLD, BOOK AND JOB P
1875.

ADVERTISEMENT.

If the question is ever asked, who is the author of this small work, the reply will be appropriate, if it be said, that such knowledge is of no consequence compared with the circumstance, that its words and thoughts may be those of substantial truth, in which lie hid the elements of great power for good; and as to this latter, the reader who will peruse it carefully and thoughtfully, from the beginning to the end, can form his own satisfactory judgment.

TO THE READER:

The object of this System of Philosophy is, to improve the condition of Man; first, by explaining the abstract theory of his construction; and, second, by showing how the theory is made practical, in virtue of this knowledge, by the harmony of action it promotes as between the desired purposes of God and the desired purposes of Man, in which combination of thought in the two kinds of Mind, consists all progress as to human life, health and happiness as to individual Men, to Nations, and to all Humanity.

These "desired purposes," united as one, are supposed to be, such a construction of the being of Man as would make him to be complete in every particular, with the view to his highest use, in thought and action, in the whole realm of responsible duty, in the place he is destined to fill in creation.

This System, in a great degree, is one of abstractions. The principal ideas are few in number, but each one fills a place in the structure that no other one can fill, and the place and existence of each is essential to a perfect combination in such a being as man. As each idea is *supposed* to be perfect in itself with the view to a specific use, so the whole combined as one, is *supposed* to be perfect in itself. Each binds the whole together, and the whole holds each in its true place of responsibility and duty. These abstract ideas are all recognized by the common mind, but the order of their combination is not well understood, and hence much power is lost in consequence of the confusion to the Mind of Man that follows action, as with an undisciplined army in battle, when confronted with one whose organization and disposition in the battle is the best possible. The power of mental truth lies in its recognition as such. That condition fulfilled, it begets truth, and thus within itself it has the elements and power of progress, as is believed to be the case with this System of Philosophy.

It is claimed for this System that its truth is demonstrated, in common sense, in all nature as a whole, and in each and every created action and thing, and should it be so recognized by Man, that the effect and use would be to him, practically, in the highest degree beneficent; for, by its power, order would encroach up n and take the place of disorder all along the line of human life, for the reason that the Human Mind would there meet the Divine Mind in truth in the processes of nature, and the weaker and less perfect would gather order and power from the stronger and the perfect, for the highest usefulness, and the result would be a gradual approximation in growth to the perfection of true proportion, morally and physically, to the attainment of all human rational usefulness and happiness in the being and destiny of Man. It is not supposed that this change will come suddenly, or with noise and commotion, but that it will be wrought as the power of secret prayer moves the Mind of God to work out his purposes of love in Man, or as the sunshine or the dews of heaven fall on the earth, and that its certain effect will be proven, from time to time, by common observation and statistical facts, as in other things.

We repeat, the System is one of abstractions, and its effect will be general rather than partial to the common observation. By it the few can affect the many, and the circle of power will widen till all can think and act in harmony. Its disposition is that of love in truth, and its order of progress that of peace. By its power, differing nations, sects and conditions will more and more wish each other well and not ill; and hatred, war, and the multitude of prejudices and vicious appetites and propensities that now work so much disorder of mind and body, in all the forms of human infirmity and misery, will grow weak in themselves, and finally disappear, as they are compelled to give place to opposing dispositions and virtues. Those forces that work together for the health and happiness of Man will be made strong, while those that work disorder, sickness and unhappiness, will grow weak and powerless in control, in similar proportion. In a word, JUSTICE and MERCY will more and more, in thought and action, harmonize together in all things, as they do in the Divine and Human in JESUS CHRIST, who ordains, that nothing that is UNJUST in Man can be MERCIFUL, and that nothing that is UNMERCIFUL in him can be JUST. And then will become to be recognized as a present fact and power, that "THE KINGDOM OF HEAVEN IS WITHIN YOU."

THE THEORY.

God is the highest possible power—Allwise and Almighty.

Man is the highest earthly creation of God, was made in his image, but is less and limited in both wisdom and power, but is sufficient in each to meet the ends of his creation and to fill the measure of his destined use.

These four abstract ideas appear to lie at the foundation of his construction, as the representative of all animated existence in Nature, to-wit:

1. Organization.
2. Perpetuation.
3. Sustenance.
4. Protection.

On examination it will be seen that these ideas are essentials, for, without Organization there could be no such a being as Man. But, in his structure, of what use would be Organization, if without duration in time, in himself, or in his species? Hence, united in organization is Perpetuation, whose office is to prolong Organization till earthly uses are accomplished. Again: How could his Organization be perpetuated in time unless constantly Sustained? Man must have air, food, water, and the power within himself to so combine the whole as to form new tissue for the body, to supply the waste or decay. Organization is Perpetuated by Sustenance, as an essential condition. There is still another abstract fundamental power, to-wit: Protection. For, all Life has its enemies that will destroy it, if they can; hence, it demands Protection from its enemies. Thus, Organization, Perpetuated by Sustenance, is Protected from its enemies; or read in the reverse order, from the external to the internal: Protection Sustains Perpetuation in Organization. Such are the differing characters of the four great instincts that bind the whole together as one Man—the mutual combination of the whole four in harmony, being essential to his completeness.

Thus, these four powers are essential ones in fundamental element, in the continued existence of Man on earth, as the representative of the excellences of all Animated Nature, to-wit:

1. The Organizing Power.
2. The Perpetuating Power.
3. The Sustaining Power.
4. The Protecting Power.

The office of the first is to Organize, the second to Perpetuate, the third to Sustain, and the fourth to Protect the abstract Man. Organization Perpetuates Sustenance by Protection; and, Protection Sustains Perpetuation by Organization.

The idea is, that these four Powers in Man are mutual friends, are the fountain of, and give character to so many instincts, so existing one within the other, in the order of their offices, that they make a perfect whole, and yet, as ideas, are in themselves distinct, each from the other. If we withdraw from Man the fourth, his Life is destroyed by its enemies. If the third be withdrawn, Man perishes of want. If the second be withdrawn, time or duration ceases with him. If the first be withdrawn, nothing of Man, in organized material structure, remains. But, if we add the first, to Man is secured the order, element and form of Life, in Species. If the second be added to this, duration of existence is provided for. If we add the third, substantial supply of those things essential to bodily support in Life is the result. If we add the fourth, Man is protected in health from those enemies that make constant war upon his Life and consequent existence here.

Thus, these four powers severally organize, perpetuate, sustain and protect each other, and all combine in Man; and they bind each to the other in harmonious form for the purposes he is designed to fill in Life. By them, he is Organized as Man in power and character. He is Perpetuated in power and character as Man. He is Sustained as Man is sustained in Life; and he is Protected from the enemies of his person and Life, by them in combination. In virtue of their order in him in Life, Character and Person, Man is Man. According to the fullness of these several powers in Man, and the completeness of their combination in him, consists his perfection in Life, Person, Character and Destiny; but, *on the condition that he obeys the voice of God speaking in his Nature*, that ever urges man, in all his actions to the attainment, in his conduct, to the highest use.

These six terms appear to constitute that Language, to-wit:

1. PRINCIPLE.
2. LAW.
3. RESULT.
4. CAUSE.
5. EFFECT.
6. USE.

Each and all of the four fundamental powers of Man, as named heretofore, to-wit: The instinct that organizes, the instinct that perpetuates, the instinct that sustains, and the instinct that protects, obey the order of action indicated by these six terms in directing power from its Principle to its Use in all that is comprehended in the CONDUCT of Man, and each and every distinct thing in Nature terminating in a use, bears their full and distinct moral impress in combination with each other in particular order, and with the four fundamental terms which they influence by CHOICE, and which four, by INSTINCT, influence them. Their numbers are but the modulations of God's voice in all created things. Man, in virtue of his creation recognizes these terms in his Character, and enunciates them in his Conduct. They enter into every thought of his mind and action of his body that terminates in a distinct use.

Thus, Man is possessed of certain *Natural Powers*, which lie at the foundation of his Character. These Natural Powers have been named, to-wit:

1. THE ORGANIZING POWER.
2. THE PERPETUATING POWER.
3. THE SUSTAINING POWER.
4. THE PROTECTING POWER.

Accordingly as he possesses fullness in these four terms, Man has the elements of a full and perfect Character as Man. Character is developed by Conduct,* by means of the Rational Faculties, and the Rational Faculties recognize and obey the order of these six terms in the attainment of every distinct purpose, thought or thing of use, to-wit:

1. PRINCIPLE.
2. LAW.
3. RESULT.
4. CAUSE.
5. EFFECT.
6. USE.

All the arrangements in the Nature of Man by which the Power of Protection Sustains the Perpetuity of his Organization, as we read him from the external to the internal; or, if read in the reverse order, by which Organization, Perpetuated by Sustenance becomes his Protection, recognize the complete order of the foregoing six terms. In the duties of human requirement Man receives all things in his Natural Powers from God in Principle, the first term of this Language, and in the sixth term—Use—he returns the power so received to him in action, in virtue of Law and Result, Cause and Effect. God speaks in our Natural Powers to our Rational Faculties in this Language in all sciences and in the processes of science, and in Man, as a whole, and in every organ, fibre and tissue, bone, nerve and muscle, that go to make up the whole. They mark the order of the action of Mind in all created being destined to a use. In that order, a Principle, by a Law, flows into a Result, which Result, in a Cause, by an Effect, flows into a Use, as we trace the flow from the internal into the external. If we commence with the sixth term, we say, a Use is the Effect of a Cause, which Cause is the Result of a Principle developed by a Law. Thus, we trace power in the order of these terms from Principle into

---

*Thus *Character* has its foundation in *Instinct*, and these terms define the elements of its structure, to-wit:

1. ORGANIZATION.
2. PERPETUATION.
3. SUSTENANCE.
4. PROTECTION.

These Powers influence human action as *Character* influences *Conduct*, but do not absolutely *govern* it, for *Conduct* is a thing of *volition* or *choice* of the Rational Faculties in Man, and the logic of its action is defined in the order of these six terms:

1. PRINCIPLE.
2. LAW.
3. RESULT.
4. CAUSE.
5. EFFECT.
6. USE.

Use, through Law, Result, Cause and Effect, by synthesis; and from Use into Principle by Effect and Cause, Result and Law, by analysis.

So, we receive power from God, in Principle, and return it to him in the Use we have made of it; whence it flows into Principle and hence again into Use. In this way the stream flows from its fountain and returns to it again; ready to commence again its perpetual flow, purified, if need be, in the Mind of God.

So, these four powers are fundamental in the existence of Man, and on them in combination is founded his CHARACTER, to-wit:

1. THE ORGANIZING POWER.
2. THE PERPETUATING POWER.
3. THE SUSTAINING POWER.
4. THE PROTECTING POWER.

In these four Powers, working in harmony, all the processes in Man are ordered, each for its special object and purpose, in the required order of these six terms, to-wit:

1. PRINCIPLE.
2. LAW.
3. RESULT.
4. CAUSE.
5. EFFECT.
6. USE.

Thus, in the order of power and place of these TEN IDEAS, to-wit: The FOUR Natural Powers named, and the SIX terms that constitute the Language of God in Nature apprehended by the Rational Faculties in Man, all the things in his construction are expressed for their special Use in Life.

A Man, full in the four fundamental Powers of Organization, Perpetuation, Sustenance and Protection, and those powers in Nature working in harmony in the construction of the human system, each and all combined to the accomplishment of the highest possible Use of each several part of the said system and of the whole combined as one, in the full force of the unerring logic and directness of a Principle, developed by Law into a Result, from an adequate Cause, by the full Effect of that Cause, would be a complete and perfect Man, for the whole ten ideas would be justly combined in his every part and in the whole, to make it so. In other words, it would be so, because it could not be otherwise, and hence, Faith.

For, in all Animated Nature these ten terms instinctively press to a combination in individuality, the effort being, for ORGANIZATION to meet its appropriate USE, the eight intermediate terms fulfilling the offices essential to the true order of the passage. If the whole work together in the fullness* of harmony, the thing formed is perfect in itself. Man being the highest of all Animated Creation, they may unite in perfect harmony and fullness in him, the highest Organization flowing to the most perfect created Use.

Into such simplicity of relation do all the seeming complexity of things resolve themselves in Nature, when we trace them in their refinement, in pure and truthful thought, and in such a frame, notice the plan and order that grasps them all; which conducts each distinct thought of God in Nature in Organization to its appointed and special Use, and there Protects it from its enemies, till its Use is accomplished in time, in the place it is appointed to fill.

Such is the abstract theory of Man. Could the People receive it in its simple form, and when they thought of Man, would they recog-in mind the ten powers and forms constantly combining in him to perfect the fullness of Use on the line of generation of new tissue, or growth, the fullness desired in full and perfect Manhood would be continually approximated, and the time of a generation would go far to work the renovation of the world of Humanity. Much of its present inharmony in Society would disappear, and much of the pain, sorrow and unhappiness from disease would be prevented, for their causes would be removed. These ten terms or ideas take hold on the living virtues of living things in the very fountains of existence, and were so planted there of God, to be so recognized of Man, and the condition of their recognition by Man as striving to attain fullness in the human construction, in the mind of God, is the condition on which fullness of Manhood can be attained.

---

*In the term "Fullness," in this connection, we mean that point of attainment in the construction of Man, as a whole, and consequently in each distinct part, where nothing is wanting to make perfect completeness with the view to the highest USE, and where nothing is redundant, which would be but added weakness.

FURTHER EXPLANATION OF THIS THEORY AND ITS PRACTICAL WORKINGS.

THE FIRST ILLUSTRATION.

Before applying the examination of this Theory of Philosophy more particularly to Man, in his construction, we would make further explanation of its general application to all the works of God, in Nature, as a whole as in every distinct part. Let us refer to the creation of the world, as revealed from heaven:

The world was created in six distinct divisions, or periods of time, called days. Each day had its peculiar work. The whole was *Organized* for *Perpetuation*, by *Sustenance*, for *Protection* in Time, in the order of Principle, Law, Result, Cause, Effect, and Use.

In the FIRST DAY was created Light as a *Principle*, reflecting the image of all Material things.

In the SECOND DAY, the Firmament was created, and the waters above and below it were divided, in accordance with the *Law* of the Principle of the Light.

In the THIRD DAY, the Dry Land was made to appear, and Vegetable Life sprang forth as a *Result* of the action and order of the Divine Mind.

In the FOURTH DAY, the Lights in the Firmaments of heaven were created, as a developing *Cause* of the Principle of Light, created on the First Day.

In the FIFTH DAY, the Fish of the sea and the Fowl of the air were created, as an *Effect* in their order, to people the Sea and the Air, the work of the Second Day.

In the SIXTH DAY were created the lower Animals and Man, to people the dry land and subsist, directly or indirectly, on vegetable life, the creation of the Third Day, as the highest *Use*.

So, that in the First Three Days, respectively, were prepared habitations and sustenance for what was created, in the order of time, on the Last Three Days.

The things created on the Fourth, Fifth and Sixth days, have an affinity for, as an inhabitant for a habitation, the things that were created, in their order, on the First, Second and Third Days.

Thus, the *Sun*, as a body, has its habitation in *Light*.

The Fish of the Sea and the Fowl of the Air have their habitation in the Waters and in the Firmament, and therein they exist.

The Lower Animals and Man have their habitation on dry land, and subsist directly or indirectly, on Vegetable Life.

In the progressive order of things, the Second Three terms of the Language of God in Nature have an affinity for the First Three, as an inhabitant for a habitation. Let us place them in the following order, to-wit:

First Three.	*Second Three.*
PRINCIPLE.	CAUSE.
LAW.	EFFECT.
RESULT.	USE.

In the world, and the Life of the world, the Sun, as a *Cause*, and Light as a *Principle*, meet and act together.

The Firmament and the Waters, and the Fish of the Sea and the Fowl of the Air, as a *Law* and its *Effect*, meet and act together.

The Dry Land and Vegetable Life, and the Lower Animals and Man, meet and act together as a *Result* and its *Use*.

This appears to be the machinery in the *Organization*, *Perpetuation*, *Sustenance* and *Protection* of the world and the things therein, as a whole.

A *Cause* meets a *Principle ;* an *Effect* meets its *Law*, and the *Result* its *Use*.

The Light that clothes the Sun, as a body, is thus united with it, as a *Cause* of action unites with its *Principle* of action, and hence the constant development of its power, and the life of all earthly things hangs upon the *Effect* of its *Law ;* hence, also, flows every consequent *Result*, for its appropriate *Use*.

There may be contained in this order of division of these six terms the image of the two Sexes, Male and Female, that are recognized in reproduction in all progressive life.

In relation to that great Use, the image of

PRINCIPLE,
LAW, and
RESULT,

may exist in the one Sex, and that of

CAUSE,
EFFECT, and
USE,

may exist in the other Sex. Progress in the reproduction of life must consist in the union of these six terms, in this order, as one, and hence the necessity of marriage, for the purpose of new *Organization* to *Perpetuate* the species of each kind of living thing by *Sustenance* for its *Protection*, is apparent.

So, we repeat, the Sun, in the movement of the world, stands in the place of a *Cause*, and the Light in the place of a *Principle*. The two are in constant union, and the *Cause* developes the *Principle* by the *Law* of the Firmament and the Waters above and under it, and Fish and Fowl exist in consequence as an *Effect* in elements suited to their natures. The Dry Land and Vegetable Life stand in the place of *Result*, for the *Use* of the Lower Animals and Man. So, in the constant generations of the things of the world, in their progressive flow, a *Cause* meets a *Principle*, a *Law* generates an *Effect*, and a *Result* provides for a *Use*, both as to the whole world, and to every distinct part.

The connection of the work of the six periods of time that span the creation of the world, may be traced in this Axiom:

The *Principle* of Light in which consists the image of all material things, by a *Law* of the Firmament, flows into Vegetable Life, in all its forms, as a *Result*; which Result, by the Sun as a *Cause*, developing in the mind and power of God, Fish and Fowl in the order of living existence, as an *Effect*, flows into the creation of the Lower Animals, and finally into Man, as the highest possible created Use.

In reconstruction of living things, the six terms of the Language of GOD in Nature may be read from the internal to the external always thus:

A *Cause* developes a *Principle*, by, or in accordance with a *Law*, hence an *Effect*, with a *Result*, for a *Use*.

Or, if read in the reverse order, from the external to the internal, the reading is:

A *Use* is the *Result* of an *Effect* of a *Law*, which, from or by a *Cause*, has developed a *Principle* of Life.

SECOND ILLUSTRATION.

In the foregoing, the order of the whole world is defined. Let us now examine the order of the action of a single part in the process of reproduction:

Here is a single kernel of wheat. Common sense, with the proof of analogy, teaches me that the kernel contains within itself the elementary power of *Organization* of new kernels, (one or many) to *Perpetuate*, to *Sustain*, and to *Protect* the Life of its species. The process of providing this is subject to certain conditions, which are,—that the *Principle* of life within the kernel be developed in the order of a particular *Law*, by the force of an adequate *Cause*, producing a specific *Effect*. The *Result* is, the germination of a new plant, bearing new kernels, (one or many) as a *Use*, in *Organizing*, *Perpetuating*, *Sustaining* and *Protecting* the life of its species, and keeping it in continued existence in the world.

Let us further illustrate the meaning and order of this process by the following supposition, which may be the true one. I have cast the seed into the earth, and thereby placed it in the power of the Chemical forces, the action of which may be this:

Oxygen.
Nitrogen.
Hydrogen.
Carbon.

Oxygen is the *Organizing* Power.
Nitrogen the *Perpetuating* Power.
Hydrogen the *Sustaining* Power.
Carbon the *Protecting* Power.

In the production of the new kernel or crop of wheat, as in every one, the following chemical forces have, in some way acted, to-wit:

LIGHT.
HEAT.
POSITIVE ELECTRICITY.
NEGATIVE ELECTRICITY.
GALVANISM.
ATTRACTION.

And in the process, these forces may have each acted towards the other as the terms,

PRINCIPLE,
LAW,
RESULT,
CAUSE,
EFFECT,
USE,

are related to each other in their action and power in all the processes of nature.

THIRD ILLUSTRATION

Mind, working in Life, in the order of

PRINCIPLE,
LAW,
RESULT,
CAUSE,
EFFECT,
USE,

For the purposes of

ORGANIZATION,
PERPETUATION,
SUSTENANCE, and
PROTECTION,

Also in its workings, combining the terms :

NOTHING,
ONE,
TWO,
THREE,
FOUR,
FIVE,
SIX,
SEVEN,
EIGHT,
NINE,

In the rule or order of

DIVISION,
MULTIPLICATION,
SUBTRACTION,
ADDITION,

counts, weighs, measures, defines and makes all quantities and proportions of Matter that enter into the Human System as a whole, and in each and every distinct part, for the Uses designed; and by the twenty-four terms, in conjunction, all the problems of Mind and Matter are accurately solved for every Use.

A FOURTH ILLUSTRATION.

Let us further illustrate the place and order of action of the ten terms that constitute what may be called the Vowels and Consonants in the Language of God in Nature in living progress by a reference to the plan of our system of Jurisprudence, the office of which is to restore order in the State or community by means of Justice, where it has been disturbed by injustice and consequent disorder, which injustice and disorder work injury to the rights and properties of Men.

The Principle of Justice resides in the People of the State as a whole, and the protection of human Life and its properties from their enemies rest upon it. But, in that form its administration would be so inconvenient as to be inoperative. Let us trace it, step by step, in its progress in and by this system to its Use in restoring the order of Justice that has been disturbed.

The several terms or ideas from and through which Justice flows from Principle into a final Use, in our system of Jurisprudence mentioned, are the following:

1. The State.
2. The Legislature.
3. The Court.
4. The Cause.
5. The Trial.
6. The Verdict.

These terms may be read as follows:

The Principal of Justice in the State, by Law of the Legislature, flows into a Court of Jurisprudence as a Result: which Result in a Cause of Action, by the Effect of a Trial, flows into a Just Verdict as a Use.

Here are six different forms in which Justice resides, from its habitation in the whole People of a State, to its specific form and use in a true and proper Verdict.

First, it resides in the State: Second it resides in the Legislature: Third, it resides in the Court: here (Fourth) Justice confronts its enemies in a Cause of action: Fifth, the Effect is, a Trial: and, Sixth, it passes into the Use of a Verdict, where Justice is restored to the community again.

To analyze and compare further the six terms of the Language of Progress in Nature, we repeat, it will be seen that there is a well defined division of the same—each division of which consists of three terms, to-wit:

FIRST, { PRINCIPLE,
LAW,
RESULT.

SECOND, { CAUSE,
EFFECT,
USE.

So, in the flow of the Principle of Justice in the State, the same division may be observed, to-wit:

FIRST, { THE STATE,
THE LEGISLATURE,
THE COURT.

SECOND, { THE CAUSE,
THE TRIAL,
THE VERDICT.

Mind, by the First Three,—

The State,
The Legislature.
The Court,

Organizes by Statute Law, the power to *Perpetuate* Justice, which is *Sustained* and *Protected* by the Second Three,—

The Cause,
The Trial,
The Verdict.

In the process, in a Cause of action, we appeal to the State; in the Trial, we appeal to the common or statute law, as enacted and defined by the Legislature; and for the Verdict, which is to restore Justice, where it has been violated, we appeal to the Court.

In this way we constantly strive to *Organize*, *Perpetuate*, *Sustain* and *Protect* the Principle and power of Justice, as applicable to each individual person, and to all alike, in the State ; and to attain this end, we recognize the six divisions of power, that, moving in their order, move all things in completeness of action, and which represent, in their several places, these universal terms : *Principle*, *Law*, *Result*, *Cause*, *Effect* and *Use*.

OF THE THEORY MORE CLOSELY APPLIED TO MAN.

Man is the highest creation in earthly being. He exists in a constitution peculiar to himself. He inhabits a material body, which is a part of himself, but only a part. The body has been examined with all the labor of patient genius, and the manner of its particular construction is well apprehended by the Rational Faculties in science. Even the abstract materials of which it is composed have been resolved into their original elements in matter, and in what it consists in more refined and delicate forms, ascertained. But, the Material Body is not all of Man. After it has been resolved into its most delicate forms of matter, it is still only Matter. Mind and Life are something else; and Mind and Life exist in man as certainly as Matter. May we not understand the order and place, respectively, of Mind and Life, as certainly as we do those of Matter?

And here we will again remark, that the nearer we approach to Deity in refinement of idea, the plainer and more simple are the laws of combination in all created things. As Man bears the image of God himself, we can look for an explanation of the plan of his living structure, conspicuous for its simplicity in general arrangement.

Man, in virtue of his place in creation, aspires to a higher state of being than mere Nature appoints to him. To accomplish this, he has certain conditions to fulfill in his own right and duty. God provides for him the helps and instruments of his ascent. It is for Man, as a *condition*, that he grasps and uses them. To do this, to use rightfully these helps, the *faith of knowledge* is an essential thing. What can a man rightly do in the construction of a house, for instance, if he has no knowledge of the foundation timbers of the same? These timbers may be few in number, compared with all those contained in the whole structure; but, inasmuch as the existence of the whole edifice rests on these few, nothing can be planned or done well till the name, place and use of these are well fixed in the faith of Mind. Let us proceed boldly, yet with caution, to the task of defining the fundamental ideas in the whole human constitution and the essential place of each, so that when we think of Man, we may just as clearly think of what is essential to his health and full development, understandingly, without disorder, and all alike.

And when we can all *think alike* of Man, in the depth of his being, we shall soon feel alike and act alike towards each other in the discharge of the great duties of life; and in a word, *be* alike in good will and good health, in mind and body. In this theory, in virtue of the joint action of the mind of God and Man, humanity will grow into greatness.

The first form of power in man is Organization, and Organization is the result of the action of Mind in Life, in Matter. Action is a property of Mind, and Inertia is a property of Matter. As matter, in itself, is inert, and cannot move except as it is moved, Mind, in action, must be its moving power. If Mind works in the order of Truth to a given end, it has this great advantage over falsehood, and consequent disorder: It has the power of God to help it, for all truth is the wisdom of God.

It is the evident condition of all Human Progress that the Faith of the Human Mind must rest on and combine in some distinct form in the Truth of God in relation to anything in which progress is to be made. If human Faith is founded in scientific knowledge, it is then so complete as not to be questioned by the Mind: for, scientific knowledge flows from the deductions of the Human Mind, combined with or resting on one or more truths of God in relation to particular things. For instance, the six mechanical powers are so many Truths of God. The Mind of man by receiving a knowledge of them, so rests on and combines in those truths in thought that the combination becomes unquestioned Faith, on which the man acts with such certainty, that he contracts to build a steam engine, for instance, of a given power of action, or such other contrivance as he chooses, and he does build the same, it having previously existed in his own Mind as a thing of Faith. So of the human constitution. The abstract powers on which it rests are Truths of God, on which human knowledge may rest and in which it can combine, and then such knowledge becomes Scientific Faith, and by that Faith of Mind, progress is made in Natural Living Organization in Life and material being, until the thing is full and complete.

Man, in the complete abstract, consists of one idea, to wit: One Man. All that is contained in Man, in his many parts, so combine as to make one perfect whole, which whole is expressed in Mind, in completeness, in one idea—Man.

But Man, in himself, contains four other ideas in which are represented fullness for the purpose designed.

1. The Organizing Power.
2. The Perpetuating Power.
3. The Sustaining Power.
4. The Protecting Power.

The first of these powers flows into the second; the first, in the the second, flows into the third, and the three interior ideas flow into and inhabit the fourth, which is the external power. The four powers in Man, possessed severally of the above offices, are these, to-wit:

1. Mind.
2. Immortal Life.
3. Mortal Life.
4. Material Body.

The first is the Organizing power in Man: the second is the Perpetuating power; the third is the Sustaining power, and the fourth is the Protecting power of Man, in his earthly existence. In other words, expressing the same thing, Mind organizes, Immortal Life perpetuates, Mortal Life sustains, and the Material Body protects the whole existence, structure and being of man on earth.

Mind, in Immortal Life, in Mortal Life, gives its external expression in the Material Body, and these four powers, acting in harmony as one being, make the Man. In these four terms, in combination, consists human selfhood, in personality. They are and have been common to all human beings that have ever existed, that exists now, or that ever will exist on the whole earth. They should exist in FULLNESS respectively and in combination—each and every part, in its interior construction and in all, acting as one with the view to any designed Use, in the order of Principle, Law, Result, Cause and Effect. And thus, heeding the same language of the Rational Faculties in Nature, in the fullness of power, in the fullness of order, and in the fullness of action in that order, every essential Use is attained and every Use is protected in its office, all pressing towards completeness in the thing designed in each organ, part and power in the construction of Man.

It is not our purpose, in this place, to treat of the deficiencies that may exist in Man in the four fundamental powers of his being, or in the combined whole, but, to define in truth what he *should be*, that he may be *made* what he should be.

And here we will repeat that Man *should be* formed of these four powers in the fullness of their offices to make him a MAN, perfect in his Selfhood, as such, intellectually, morally and physically, to-wit: in

1. The ORGANIZING Power.
2. The PERPETUATING Power.
3. The SUSTAINING Power.
4. The PROTECTING Power.

These several Powers in Man are:

1. MIND.
2. IMMORTAL LIFE.
3. MORTAL LIFE.
4. MATERIAL BODY.

If these powers in the individual man are full, he is *full* in SOUL or character, and as such, is answerable to God in the discharge of all responsible duty, to himself, to his neighbor, to his species and to society. His Rational Faculties would obey the order of his Natural Powers in Principle, Law, Result, Cause and Effect in the attainment of every distinct Use that exists in or proceeds from the Material Body, as the Personal Protecting power, on earth of his Mortal Life, his Immortal Life and his Mind.

Such is the power and quality of the human Mind, that if this idea is clearly apprehended in the force of scientific Faith, if it be determined that these four conditions shall be full and complete *on the line of generation*, they will be; for the Mind of God and Man would unite therein to make it so—and hence, completeness in the fundamental elements of character. In that way can be laid a large, broad, tough and enduring *Personality* in Men and Nations, which character should be developed in CONDUCT in the Providence of God and Man.

Man, in virtue of his being MAN, has certain duties and responsibilities that he owes, UNDER GOD, to himself, as Male and Female, to his Species, and to Society. By Society, we mean, all those organizations wherein men unite for mutual protection in well-being, as Families and Nations.

It is the order of Nature, that all Mortal Life must die, and the Material Body, its habitation, decay; yet, Man, in his Species, continues in Perpetuity. In individual personality, Men disappear from earth, one after another, till all who have lived at any given point of time are gone from earthly existence. Yet their descendants live in the family, in nations, and in the species. The family, the nation, and the species are each and all composed of individual persons. Individual persons all die, but those societies of which the individual persons compose the whole, may continue to exist, in virtue of the order in Nature of the Sustaining power of the Providence of God, in Male, Female and Offspring. For Man, in himself, has the power of reproduction; of furnishing to his species new beings like himself in general conformation and personality, and thus the increase of human beings supplies the waste caused by death, and thus is kept in life and responsibility on earth the species of Man.

This supply of the species with new human beings, to take the place of those who pass away by death, comes of generation. The four constituents of Personality, in its fullness have been named. New generation supposes new Personality, distinct from the old, as one unit is distinct from another unit, but possessed of like constituent elements, in fundamental structure.

In the order of things in relation to Man in this progressive flow of the stream of Life four great ideas exist, around which all things revolve, or from which all progress is evolved, and they are named as follows—and they are related to each other in the order in which they stand, as numbered, from the internal to the external, to-wit:

1. FAITH.
2. TIME.
3. OFFSPRING.
4. DIVINE JUSTICE.

These appear to be the fundamental powers of human Consciousness in the Soul of Man, that enable him to apprehend the right of every useful thing, and to recognize the wrong. In combination they are the guide of Moral Action, directing the Soul, by the Rational Faculties, to distinguish and to attain each and every rational Use, touching every responsible human duty, by Principle, Law, Result, Cause and Effect.

Faith, in Time, in Offspring, is Protected in Divine Justice.

1. Faith is the ORGANIZING POWER.

2. Time is the PERPETUATING POWER.

3. Offspring is the SUSTAINING POWER.

4. Divine Justice is the PROTECTING POWER in the Conscience of Man, in all things relating to himself, to his neighbor, to his species, and to God. If these four powers are full and perfect in the individual Man, the one operating in the other as an inhabitant in its habitation, Conscience will ever be in the Soul of man a voice of warning urging him to do that which is right and dissuading him from that which is wrong, in all things that relate to himself, to his Neighbor, to his Species, and to God, in all responsible duty in Life and conduct.

We have now defined the conditions and order of full MANHOOD, and also the conditions of a full CONSCIENCE in that Manhood. In the full Soul we have an *Actor*, and in the full Conscience, a *Guide* to right action, and both equal in power to discharge the duties of the office to which they are appointed severally to fill. In all the actions of Life, Conscience points Man to the *Use* of the action as the object of duty, and Principle, Law, Result, Cause and Effect are represented in the *Use* of every action.

The highest Use in Nature to which Conscience can point is the Organization, Perpetuation, Sustenance and Protection of Man in the fullness of his power, in his species, which powers are represented in a new human being, in

1. NEW MIND.
2. NEW IMMORTAL LIFE.
3. NEW MORTAL LIFE.
4. NEW MATERIAL BODY.

But, in progressive life, in the order of Nature, the Use in a thing is dependent on previous action, and there are four actions in which all humanity rest, and by which, as conditions, they have existed since the first creation in Adam. The names of these actions or ideas are as follows, to-wit :

1. MARRIAGE.
2. CONCEPTION.
3. GESTATION.
4. BIRTH.

1. Marriage is the *Organizing* Action.
2. Conception is the *Perpetuating* Action.
3. Gestation is the *Sustaining* Action.
4. Birth is the *Protecting* Action of the species of Man, in generation, in the order of Nature, and ever must be. They relate to each other as the four powers of Manhood, or as the four fundamental powers of Conscience relate to each other—their power grasps all humanity in Natural action, as the second four do in Conscience, or the first four in Purpose. The first four are these:

1. MIND.
2. IMMORTAL LIFE.
3. MORTAL LIFE.
4. MATERIAL BODY.

In these four is contained the desire and purpose of new human being, to supply the waste of the species caused by death.

The second four are these:

1. FAITH.
2. TIME.
3. OFFSPRING.
4. DIVINE JUSTICE.

In these four, in combination, consists the *Conscience* that directs and holds all essential action flowing from that purpose to its fullness in specific Use,—the completeness of Man on the line of generation.

The third four are these, in which the *Purpose*, in the *Conscience*. is expressed in Action, in the order of Nature, for the Sustenance of the Species of Man, to-wit:

1. MARRIAGE.
2. CONCEPTION.
3. GESTATION.
4. BIRTH.

In the first four consists the power of *purpose*; in the second four consists the power of *right order* in that purpose; in the third four consists the power of purpose in the order of *Natural action.* In the first four is *Organization ;* in the second four is *Perpetuation ;* in the third four is *Sustenance*, and in a fourth four, which is the image of the first four in name, but distinct in person, to-wit:

1. New Mind.
2. New Immortal Life.
3. New Mortal Life.
4. New Material Body,

is the *Protection* of the Species of Man.

The last term, it will be seen, is the *representative* of the other fifteen in combination, for the power of all have flown into it. In it are represented the *Personality* of Man, and all his rights in himself, and also, all his duties and responsibilities in and to his Species. Hence, in the weakness of the infant child is represented the Life and existence of the Species of Man, in all his thought and power, to be developed in the order of Nature, in the course of time.

The Sixteen ideas are these, to wit:

1. Mind.	1. Faith.	1. Marriage.	1. New Mind.
2. Immortal Life.	2. Time.	2. Conception.	2. New Immortal Life
3. Mortal Life.	3. Offspring.	3. Gestation.	3. New Mortal Life.
4. Material Body.	4. Divine Justice.	4. Birth.	4. New Material Body.

The first of these families *Organizes*, the second *Perpetuates*, the third *Sustains*, and the fourth *Protects* the Species of Man on earth.

In the first four consists *Personality ;* in the second four consists *right order of action* with the object of new personality ; in the third four consists right action, so purposed and so ordered : in the fourth four consists new Personality.

From *fullness* in the first four, in *fullness* in the second four, by *fullness* in third four, proceeds *fullness* in the fourth four.

These conditions being fulfilled, in the infant child would be contained the elements of a perfect Manhood. If in one infant child, why not in all? If in all, there would exist at the beginning the elements of a most profound destiny in the world of Man. When a child was thus born into the world, he would have in his favor, those abstract fundamental powers on which human greatness in usefulness is built in life and character in the physical and moral world. In his very nature he would be possessed of great breadth of synthesis, to be developed in due time, by a proportioned depth of analysis in life and actions and experiences. He would have, in Temperament, a substantial foundation in the Government of the Providence of God, whereon to build a structure worthy of the name of Man. In this way will the wisdom and power of God help the Faith of Man to perfect humanity in the highest possible form of Truth and beauty of proportion, and in substantial greatness.

It is seen, that by this theory, the foundation powers on which human nature rests in Man are laid *before the child is born into the world ;* or, at any rate, before the new being has any duty or responsibility in virtue of itself. How, then, is any force to be exercised, or to be brought to bear, so as to make that full that were otherwise deficient? This responsibility and duty rests with others, in proportion to the light given them in relation thereto. There is a great abstract power that we call the PUBLIC MIND, that seems to consist of the *average force* of a whole community of mind touching any one thing. It is the general average in a nation of all of its *organizing* power, all of its *perpetuating* power, all of its *sustaining* power, and all of its *protecting* power, the same as if it were represented in one Man, in one Mind, in one Faith. It is not the general average of the *organizing* power alone—the *Mind* of Man—but, it is that of the four great powers of Man, combined in the Material Body, the Protecting power, and all of which, if full, make the full Man. If it be thought that all virtue consists in improving the *Mind* to its full extent in a Nation, the effect will be that the powers that guard its Perpetuation, its Sustenance and its Protection will become emasculated and weak in proportion as injustice has been done them. But, this *general average*, we repeat, is that of the sum of the whole four powers combined, as they exist in the proportionate fullness or weakness of a nation. It is true, that Mind in Man is the opening door, but it is only to one of the four apartments, and it is the welcome visitor of all the rest, and the constant inhabitant. So, this *Public Mind* that we speak of is the average Mind of the *Public Manhood*—the Soul. What is wanted is, to make this full in its four-fold character, and yet, complete in its oneness of person in being and action, so that there may flow from this Public Mind of a Nation's Manhood, a great and powerful Public Faith, which will become the Organizing power of Man in Time as the Perpetuating power, in Offspring as the Sustaining power, and in Divine Justice as the Protecting power of the Manhood of the Nation. If Faith in these four powers be full, in a Nation, it will be possessed of the elements of vast and enduring greatness. It would act on the whole line of generation as a decree of heaven to be executed on earth, in the force of a great destiny, for God and Man would work together to the same great end of human exaltation and happiness.*

In nothing can we accomplish much without a purpose of what we want to do clearly defined in the Mind, and the more full and clear the purpose, the more certain we are of its accomplishment. The purpose must be *right* in itself. The *power* of its accomplishment sufficient, and the *order* of its accomplishment true. For instance, we wish to build up a Nation great in all its elements, to-wit: In *organization*, in the power of *duration*, in the power to *sustain* itself, and in the power to *protect* itself. The human Mind is so constituted that it cannot consider each individual of a Nation singly by himself, though it can include the millions in a Nation, in a single idea, and by thinking of the Nation in its oneness, can conceive of it as it should be in fullness, the same as if it were one individual person, and in this way, may think of and affect every one included in the whole. For, we can think of a Nation as a whole with the same ease and distinctness as we can think of *one Man* as a whole; and we can as clearly recognize the fact, and feel that a NATION should be possessed of fullness in all the true elements of Organization, Perpetuation, Sustenance and Protection, as we can that a single individual should be so; and, also, that this fullness is to be developed as a USE from Principle, Law and Result, Cause and Effect.

By the recognition of this theory in this simple form of thought, the Mind of Man will coincide with the Mind of God in truth, and the effect would be, Man would approximate to full and true Manhood,

---

*In stating this condition of National Progress, by the perfection of the individual Man, we do not invent, but describe only what now exists. It is this power of Public Faith that makes us to feel that a child born in England or Scotland will partake of the peculiarities of the Englishman or the Scotchman, and this feeling is proof of the Faith. It makes the Frenchman the Frenchman, as we see him, and it makes and keeps the Jew the Jew, and so of all others. We here simply show the Cause of these national phenomena in Nature, and how the *Cause* meeting and developing the *Principle* by its own essential *Law*, can *Effect* a *Result* for this highest possible *Use*, and fix its own peculiar *Organization*, as a nation, its own power of *Perpetuation*, as such, its own power of *Sustenance*, and its own power of *Protection*.

and Nations of Men would approximate to full and true Nationality. in the power of—

1. ORGANIZATION.
2. PERPETUATION.
3. SUSTENANCE, and
4. PROTECTION.

Moved in the order of—

1. PRINCIPLE.
2. LAW.
3. RESULT.
4. CAUSE.
5. EFFECT.
6. USE.

OF THE FOUR FUNDAMENTAL IDEAS OF CONSCIENCE.

In the order of things, four great ideas permeate and include all organized thought, all perpetuity of action, all sustenance of living progress, and all protection of the Material Body in Man, to-wit:

1. Faith.
2. Time.
3. Offspring.
4. Divine Justice.

Faith Organizes, Time Perpetuates, Offspring Sustains, and Divine Justice Protects Man in all the world of thought and action. These ideas balance all conduct in truth, in relation to all things of moral movement.

They fix the character and regulate the conduct of Man, for his best good, in all things relating to Himself, to his Neighbor and to God.

For the best good of Man in Himself, of Man in his Neighbor, of Man in Society, and of Man in his relation to Deity, they fix his character and regulate his conduct. The Uses of Faith, the Uses of Time, the Uses of Offspring, and the Uses of Divine Justice, are results that are the essentials of all progress in the moral and physical being of Man. They are the fountain and foundation of the human Conscience, and if the Man be full in the conception and knowledge of these four ideas, his Conscience will be right as to all essential things. To explain this more completely, let us examine each with a clear and substantial analysis, taking the terms in the order in which they stand.

OF FAITH.

The great organizing power of Man, is Mind. The great perpetuating power of *Mind*, in relation to other things, is *Faith*, or Mind, organized in thought. in the logic of conscious Truth. Faith is the Result of the action of Mind as a Principle, developed by Volition as a Law, combining in or with certain truths of God, fixed for Man's special Use, so that he can cling to them with unerring certainty, as far as those truths are concerned. He must, as a condition, embrace those truths of God in clearness of thought, with the view to an object or distinct purpose. Take, for instance again, the six mechanical powers, to-wit: The Lever, the Plane, the Wedge, the Axle, the Pulley and the Screw. These are six truths of God. Man combines them with the view to effect some purpose. The truths are thoughts of God. The combination of them to effect the purpose is the work of the Mind of Man. The two powers, (those of God and those of man), make Faith, and from the union flows power, proportioned to the fulfillment of the purpose. The essential steps with the mechanical powers can be calculated by numbers, with mathematical exactness, and the result is, *Mathematical Faith*. This has been demonstrated as truth in the Mind by means of the four fundamental rules of Number combining the nine digits and the cypher.

What we want is, *Moral Faith*, with the view to particular Use. Hence, we say, if Man be organized for his highest Use, as man; if that perfect organization be permeated with the power of Perpetuation. and if the two have the power of Sustenance, and the three have the power of Protection, binding them altogether as one; and if the whole has been done in the unerring logic of a Principle, imbued with the virtue of full Manhood, and this Principle of fullness, developed by a full and perfect Law to that end, flows into a full and perfect Result, in virtue of a full and adequate Cause, producing a like Effect, and reaching and filling its complete intended Use,—we say, these conditions being fulfilled, we have full Moral Faith that the living thing formed will be imbued with all the powers and qualities of complete

Manhood, evolved from the original Principle. The ten ideas ending in the great Use are truths of God. The recognition of them, as working together in this logical order of truth in fullness of power to the desired end, is the office of Man, and the union of the two, (the wisdom of God and the knowledge of Man), beget, on the line of generation, the fullness that God *would* have, and Man *may* have, in the growing up of a perfect Manhood. The consciousness that those with whom rests the power to do this thing are *willing* to do it; that the *power* to do it is sufficient; that its *action* is efficient, and that the *order of its action* as a directing guide is equal to its full accomplishment in its place in Time, are essentials of the Faith of Man in its accomplishment.

Man being the highest and most perfect of all earthly created beings, Faith in the power of his reproduction in completeness, on the line of generation, full in the four fundamental powers of his character and in the power of their development, in the order of the six terms of the Language of God in Nature, in Time, is the highest form of Human Faith.

There appear to be Twenty-four essential ideas fundamental to the reproduction of a new human being—twenty-three of which flow into a twenty-fourth—Birth of a Mortal, Immortal, Mortal and Material Man.

Each and everything of living Faith must be combined in Faith, with the view to special Use; consequently, these ten terms must be employed thereby or therein: The Organizing power, the Perpetuating power, the Sustaining power, and the Protecting power. Also, Principle, Law, Result, Cause, Effect and Use. For in the construction of each living thing, that it may challenge full Faith in the Mind, it must be *organized* in Truth. It must be put together on some true plan with the view to its ultimate Use. It must be *Perpetuated* in Truth, for what is true now, is true forever in relation to that thing. It must be Sustained in the logic of Truth, and Protected by Truth, so that no falsehood can by any means enter in to destroy it. In all this, the Principle of Truth in every action must be developed by the Law of Truth that it may flow into a true Result. It must have been moved by a true and sufficient Cause, producing a true and efficient Effect, in order to reach the consummation of its true and appointed

Use. In this it is seen how the ten terms have each an inevitable and appropriate place in the Faith that we entertain in relation to the construction of Man, and each and every organ and part of Man.

In the reproduction of new human beings for the protection of Man in his species, these twenty-four terms are essential to human Faith. If any one of them is omitted, the machinery is imperfect or weak ; it would work a weakness and imperfection in the whole, for the proportion of power, or its flow, would be impaired in consequence. The terms are these, divided into six families of four terms each, to-wit :

1.	2.	3.
1. Mind,	1. Volition,	1. Faith,
2. Immortal Life,	2. Reason,	2. Time,
3. Mortal Life,	3. Common Sense,	3. Offspring,
4. Material Body.	4. Government.	4. Divine Justice.

4.	5.	6.
1. Number,	1. Love of the Sexes,	1. Marriage,
2. Language,	2. Growth,	2. Conception,
3. Power,	3. Proportion,	3. Gestation,
4. Creation.	4. Material Form.	4. Birth.

These six families, as they are numbered, flow into each other as—

1. PRINCIPLE.
2. LAW.
3. RESULT.
4. CAUSE.
5. EFFECT.
6. USE.

The Principle of the First, by the Law of the Second, flows into the Third as a Result ; which Result in the Fourth family as a Cause, by the Fifth as an Effect, flows into the Sixth, as a Use, in the Organization of the species of Man.

By taking the several terms in their order, reading from left to right, by the combinations of this Language, four grand Axioms are expressed.

Thus, by taking all the ideas numbered one, in the several families, and arranging them as below, we have the following terms or ideas :

1. MIND.
2. VOLITION.
3. FAITH.
4. NUMBER.
5. LOVE OF THE SEXES.
6. MARRIAGE.

By reading them as individual members of the several six families in the Language of Nature, by which Principle is conducted to Use, we have the following Axiom :

The Principle of Mind, by the Law of Volition, flows into Faith as a Result: which Result, in Number, (as of the sexes), as a Cause, by the Love of the Sexes as an Effect, flows into Marriage of the Sexes as a Use.

To obtain the Second Axiom, we take all the terms or Ideas numbered two, and arrange them in similar order, as in the following :

1. IMMORTAL LIFE.
2. REASON.
3. TIME.
4. LANGUAGE.
5. GROWTH.
6. CONCEPTION.

AXIOM 2. The Principle of Immortal Life, by the Law of Reason, flows into existence in Time as a Result: which Result in the Language of Nature as a Cause, by Growth as an Effect, flows into Conception as a Use.

To obtain the Third Axiom, we take all the terms or Ideas numbered three, and place them in the order in which we have placed the others, as follows, to-wit :

1. Mortal Life.
2. Common Sense.
3. Offspring.
4. Power.
5. Proportion.
6. Gestation.

Axiom 3. The Principle of Mortal Life, by the Law of Common Sense, flows into Offspring as a Result: which Result in Power as a Cause, by Proportion as an Effect, flows into new being in Gestation as a Use.

The Fourth Axiom is obtained by taking all the terms numbered Four, arranged in their regular order, as below, to-wit:

1. Material Body.
2. Government.
3. Divine Justice.
4. Creation.
5. Form.
6. Birth.

Axiom 4. The Principle of the Material Body, by the Law of its Government, flows into Offspring as a Result: which result in Creation as a Cause, by Form as an Effect, flows into the Birth of a new Human Being as a Use.

Of the four families of six terms each, in the order assigned above, the *First* is the *Organizing* Power in its relation to the other three, to-wit:

1. Mind.
2. Volition.
3. Faith.
4. Number.
5. Love of the Sexes.
6. Marriage.

The second family of six terms has the office of *Perpetuation*, to-wit:

1. IMMORTAL LIFE.
2. REASON.
3. TIME.
4. LANGUAGE.
5. GROWTH.
6. CONCEPTION.

The third family of six terms has the office of *Sustenance*, to-wit:

1. MORTAL LIFE.
2. COMMON SENSE.
3. OFFSPRING.
4. POWER.
5. PROPORTION.
6. GESTATION.

The fourth family of six terms has the office of *Protection*, to-wit:

*1. MATERIAL BODY.
2. GOVERMMENT.
3. DIVINE JUSTICE.
4. CREATION.
5. FORM.
6. BIRTH.

In the production of the new human being the Material Body of the parent is its *Protection* on the line of *Principle.*

Government is its *Protection* on the line of *Law.*

Divine Justice is its *Protection* on the line of *Result.*

Creation is its *Protection* on the line of *Cause.*

Form is its *Protection* on the line of *Effect.*

Birth is its *Protection* on the line of *Use.*

---

*We now place these terms in another form, to-wit:

Principle.	Material Body.	*Cause.*	Creation.
Law.	Government.	*Effect.*	Form.
Result.	Divine Justice	*Use.*	Birth.

In reproduction, the terms may be read into each other as follows, to-wit:

The Power of Creation of new being as a *Cause*, developing the *Principal* of new life in the Material Body by the *Law* of its Government, gives new Form as the *Effect*. The *Result* is Divine Justice in reference thereto, and the Birth of a new human Mortal and Immortal being, to perpetuate the life of the species of Man, as the *Use*.

In that way, all the other families may be read, the several terms making sense and defining their several places in reproduction.

Birth is thus a grand *Protecting Use* of Man in his Personality and of Man in his Species.

Thus, in the progress of Life, all the twenty-four terms of the foregoing combination, for the purposes above, concentrate and issue in the last term, Birth.

Birth is the door through which all the human beings that have lived since our first parents have entered into this world of action, duty and responsibility, in individual consciousness of Soul, and all who will enter it, must come in the same way. Can we not believe, with the same certainty of Faith, that the new human being, on his first breathing existence in this world, may be possessed in himself of all the elements of fullness, in all the parts of himself, defined in the order of God and recognized in the Rational Faculties of Man, whereby the full Organizing power, the full [Perpetuating power, the full Sustaining power and the full Protecting power, in Principle, Law, Result, Cause and Effect defend from its enemies a full and perfect *Use* of Manhood. As man is the highest form of earthly creation, this practical Result of endowment with fullness would be and is the highest form of Human Faith.

Man, full in his Organization, Perpetuation, Sustenance and Protection, developed in every part in Principle, Law, Result, Cause, Effect and Use, is a truth of God. The Mind of Man can apprehend this truth, and combine in it in like truth, and this is Faith in relation to this thing. According to the clearness of this Faith in the Public Mind of a Nation, will be the fullness of Power and the fullness of the expression of that power in and by the Rational Faculties in science, in art, and in true and permanent civilization, and in the health and well being of those individually who compose that Nation. In other words, it would be the Faith in a full and perfect *Manhood*, developed into a complete practical Use.

OF TIME.

We have treated of FAITH as the *Organizing* power of Mind. Let us now speak of *Time* as the Perpetuating power of Man in his Life and in all things pertaining to its constant flow. In every required action in organization the Mind has *Faith in Time.* In the least possible, as well as the greatest possible motion in Matter a certain definite portion of Time is required in which to perform it, which portion may be defined by Number, in Mathematical Faith. The fundamental powers of Number are these, to-wit:

1. NOTHING.
2. UNITY.
3. ADDITION.
4. SUBTRACTION.
5. MULTIPLICATION.
6. DIVISION.

For by these six terms, Faith of Mind organizes all things in Man with a view to perpetuation. By these ideas, Faith in the Principle of Nothing, or space, by the Law of Unity, Adds, Subtracts, Multiplies and Divides, each for its special Use, the substances that enter into the construction of the human Body. It weighs and measures each and every particle with the exactness of Number, which particles are each, one by one, transported to the place in the body where wanted, in a certain portion of Time, for healthful Use: for they move in the process by the order of the Language of God in Nature, which Language consists of these terms, to-wit:

1. PRINCIPLE.
2. LAW.
3. RESULT.
4. CAUSE.
5. EFFECT.
6. USE.

As in Number all things in Time are *Organized* in Man, so, in this Language they are *Perpetuated.*

But, Perpetuity in Time must be *Sustained* in its office, which is done by these six terms, to-wit:

1. ORDER.
2. OBEDIENCE.
3. INHABITANT.
4. HABITATION.
5. CONTROL.
6. DEFENCE.

All that is organized in truth by Faith in Number, and is Perpetuated in Language, is *Sustained* by these last six terms in the work of their offices. Not a particle of Matter is divided from other particles, in virtue of the first six terms, or is moved to its Use in virtue of the second six, but is *Sustained* on its way to and in that Use in virtue of the third six terms. Order is essential to the attainment in Nature of any Use. But, how can there be Order, without Obedience? Or how Obedience without an Inhabitant to Obey? An Inhabitant must have a Habitation in Life; and an Inhabitant in Life must have the power of Control, and the Use of Control is Defence from enemies, in whatever form they come, in Time.

The fourth family of six terms in the analysis of Time are these, to-wit:

1. MIND.
2. ACTION.
3. LIFE.
4. MATTER.
5. INERTIA.
6. TIME.

All the things of earth are contained in these six terms, to-wit:

1. MIND.
2. LIFE.
3. MATTER.

Action is a property of Mind. Inertia is a property of Matter. Action is the opposite of Inertia.

Time is evolved by the motion of matter; and the motion of matter is evolved by the action of mind overcoming its inertia. The action of mind strives to overcome the inertia of matter for the Uses of Life. The inertia of matter resists. In the contest, the action of mind overcomes the inertia of matter, but the resistance of inertia modifies the action of mind, and thus Time is evolved for each specific Use, in the order of Principle, Law, Result, Cause and Effect. Thus, the whole human body and each distinct part thereof, in its organization, perpetuation, sustenance and protection, is kept in the fullness of health in life in accordance with the evolution of Time by the motion of matter, suitable to the complete formation ot each and every part. A portion of food, for instance, is taken into the stomach. It is there divided and sent each different substance of which it is composed to its appropriate place of use,—some part goes to the formation of bone, some of muscle, and so of other constituent parts of the body. Each portion is carried to its place of final use, in a definite portion of Time, in virtue of the fact, that the action of Mind has overcome the constant disposition of Inertia of Matter to a state of rest, and this disposition of Inertia has affected and modified the action of Mind in such a way, that the particle reaches the exact spot designed in the exact time demanded for its purpose in building up the body, and in protecting it in the fullness of health in those parts that have passed off, having accomplished their appointed uses and retired to give place to others in the same office. So of every action of the human body.

So of the formation of new beings, springing from the old, differing in personality, but the same in substance, and bearing the same image; and which in time, are separated from those that bear them, as the ripe fruit falls in due time from the parent tree.

I propose to raise my arm, and do *raise it.* In doing this, the *Action* of Mind has overcome the *Inertia* of Matter. A *Use* has been *Effected* by a *Cause*, which Cause was the *Result* of some *Law*, developing a *Principle.* In the contest between the *Action* of Mind and the *Inertia* of Matter as to which shall overcome the other, *Time* is evolved in a certain proportion adapted to the purposed use.

In all this, Mind is the *Organizing* power in the purpose; the *Action* of Mind is the Perpetuating power of the purpose; *Inertia* is the *Sustaining* power, by modifying Action and securing the due pro portion of *Time* in the movement of the Matter of the Arm, with a view to the Use of the action; Matter itself, of the Arm, is the *Protecting* power of the whole.

So, of every motion of the human body, whether it be voluntary or involuntary, whether the motion be of the whole body, or that of the least pulsation thereof.

In this simple action are employed

1. The *Organizing* power of Mind.
2. The *Perpetuating* power of Action.
3. The *Sustaining* power of Inertia.
4. The *Protecting* power of Matter.

The whole has been perfected in its purposed *Use*, by

1. PRINCIPLE.
2. LAW.
3. RESULT.
4. CAUSE.
5. EFFECT.

In this way is formed every part and tissue of the human body in Life. Every particle of Matter intended for some use in building up the body is weighed and measured by Mind with a view to that use, in definite proportion and quantity, defined by Number, and the action of removing it to its place and incorporating it with the body as a part thereof, is proportioned and guaged by Time, with the view to the use of the whole, and its protection.

The Twenty-four terms that combine to make Time a great Protecting Use, in the highest created earthly being, with the view to his Organization, Perpetuation, Sustenance and Protection, in person and in his species, are these, to-wit:

1. Nothing,	1. Principle,	1. Order.	1. Mind,
2. Unity,	2. Law,	2. Obedience,	2. Action,
3. Addition,	3. Result,	3. Inhabitant,	3. Life,
4. Subtraction,	4. Cause,	4. Habitation,	4. Matter,
5. Multiplication,	5. Effect,	5. Control,	5. Inertia.
6. Divison,	6. Use.	6. Defence.	6. Time.

These terms, in their respective divisions, may each be read in the Language of God in Nature, (which is the second family in the whole combination,) and an Axiom of Common Sense expressed, to-wit:

AXIOM 1.—The Principle of Nothing, or space, by the Law of Unity, flows into Addition as a Result, in the progress of Life in generation: which Result in Substraction as a Cause, by Multiplication as an Effect, terminates in the Division of a New being from the parent stock in Birth as a Use.

Axiom 2.—Principle, by Law flows into Result—which Result in Cause, by Effect, flows into Use, and this is the Language of God in living Nature, in Time.

Axiom 3.—The Principle of Order, by the Law of Obedience, flows into the Inhabitant in Life as a Result—which Result in the Habitation of Life, (the Material Body), as a Cause, by its Control as an Effect, flows into its Defence as a Use.

Axiom 4.—The Principle of Mind, by the Law of its Action, flows into Life as a Result: which Result in Matter as a Cause, by Inertia as an Effect, flows into Time, by evolution, as a Great Protecting Use in the Organization, Perpetuation, Sustenance and Protection of Man, in his person and in his Species.

The last two families may be read into each other as follows, in Common Sense:

From *Order* in *Mind*, by *Obedience* in *Action*, flows on Inhabitant in Life: From *Habitation*, in *Matter*, by the *Control* of *Inertia*, flows *Defence* in *Time* of the being of Man.

The three families of six terms, as below, can be read into each other in order as follows, and an Axiom in Nature educed:

The *Principle* of *Order* in *Mind*, by *Law* of *Obedience* in *Action*, *Results* in an *Inhabitant* in Life: Which from *Habitation* in *Matter* as a *Cause*, by *Control*, of *Inertia* as an *Effect*, flows *Defense* in *Time* as a *Use*.

Or, the four Families may be read into each other, as follows:

The *Principle* of *Nothing* (or space,) in the *Order* of *Mind*, by the *Law* of *Unity* in *Obedience* of *Action*, *Results* in *Addition* of an *Inhabitant* in *Life:* From *Subtraction* as a *Cause* of a *Habitation* in *Matter*, with the *Multiplication* of *Control* of *Inertia* as an *Effect*, flows the *Division* of a new being from the Parent Stock in *Time* as a *Use*.

OF OFFSPRING.

The third great combination of Twenty-four terms, in this special connection. is Offspring. Faith in Time flows into Offspring, in the order of Nature in the perpetual progress of organized Life in the Species, of which latter *Offspring* is the *Sustaining* power. The twenty-four terms, in four families of six terms each, are disposed as follows, to-wit:

1st.	2d.	3d.	4th.
Soul,	Mouth,	Respiratory System,	Self,
Senses,	Stomach,	Alimentary System,	Neighbor,
Passions,	Bowels,	Osseous System,	Species,
Sympathy,	Lungs,	Mental System,	Male,
Will,	Heart,	Nervous System,	Female,
Judgment,	Blood,	Muscular System,	Offspring.

The first of these families combined is the *Organizing* power of Man in his Personality, and hence, of his Species, with a view to *Sustenance* of the whole.

The second family is the *Perpetuating* power for the same object, with a view to the Sustenance of Man, in himself and in his Species.

The third family is the *Sustaining* power of the Sustaining power for the same great Use.

The fourth family is the *Protecting* power of the *Sustaining* power of Man in himself and in his Species.

The first family of six terms in this combination is that of *Organization*, and is as follows:

1. The Soul.
2. The Senses.
3. The Passions.
4. The Sympathies.
5. The Will.
6. The Judgment.

The *Soul* occupies the place of *Principle.*
The *Senses* occupy the place of *Law.*
The *Passions* occupy the place of *Result.*
The *Sympathies* occupy the place of *Cause.*
The *Will* occupies the place of *Effect.*
The *Judgment* occupies the place of *Use.*

In combined action these may be read thus:

The *Sympathies,* as a *Cause,* meeting and developing the *Principle* of the *Soul,* by the *Law* of the *Senses,* flows into the *Will,* as an *Effect.* The *Result* is the *Passions,* for the *Use* of the *Judgment.*

The *Organizing* power expresses itself in the *Perpetuating* power, in human Personality, which latter power consists of these six terms, to-wit:

1. The Mouth.
2. The Stomach.
3. The Bowels.
4. The Lungs.
5. The Heart.
6. The Blood.

These are the organs of the Man, by which his own Life is Perpetuated in the Material Body by Sustenance, and by which, in Offspring, Life is Perpetuated in the Species. Were either of these organs omitted, no new tissue could be formed for the supply of the place of the old whose use has been accomplished, having served its time. Or, if any of them were impaired or weakened so that their office could not be well fulfilled, the action of the whole would be affected in their harmonious order, in conducting power from its Principle into its Use, in thus perpetuating the structure of the Material Body in continual fullness.

The Mouth *Perpetuates* Organization of Mind on the line of *Principle.*

The Stomach perpetuates on the line of *Law.*
The Bowels perpetuate on the line of *Result.*
The Lungs perpetuate on the line of *Cause.*
The Heart perpetuates on the line of *Effect.*
The Blood perpetuates on the line of *Use.*

All the actions of the six organs, in their natural relations to the healthy order of the Body, have a distinct relation to Faith in Time, in the production of new tissue for oneself, or of Offspring.

In reproduction; in the Sustenance of Life, in constant Action, the six terms may be read into one another in this order, to-wit:

The Lungs as a *Cause*, develope the *Principle* of the Mouth, by the *Law* of the Stomach, for *Effect* in the Heart. The Bowels occupy the place of *Result*, for the *Use* of the Blood,—the Habitation of Life.

The *Sustaining* Power of both the *Organizing* and *Perpetuating* Powers, in this combination, consists in the six Systems of Man in his individual person, to-wit:

1. The Respiratory System.
2. The Alimentary System.
3. The Osseous System.
4. The Mental System.
5. The Nervous System.
6. The Muscular System.

The Respiratory System *Sustains* the life and structure of Man by receiving the air we breathe by the Mouth and Nostrils into the Lungs. It divides the Oxygen thereof from the Nitrogen, and by the Organizing and Perpetuating powers, conducts each to its appropriate Use by the Lungs into the Blood. *Combustion* is a property of Oxygen, as Action is a property of Mind. In Nitrogen a property exists that is *the opposite* in Effect from the combustion of Oxygen, as Inertia in Matter is the opposite of the Action of Mind. Wherever there is healthful organization in Life in Man, there is also discovered the presence of Nitrogen. The combustion of Oxygen is modified by the quality opposed to combustion in Nitrogen, otherwise the tissues of the human body in the process of formation would be destroyed by burning up, instead of being formed and kept perfect for Use in Life. In the Respiratory System, the anti-combustive power in Nitrogen so modifies the combustion of Oxygen, that the pressure of both, in due proportion meeting each other in each and in every part, *Sustains Life* by furnishing a due proportion of heat to every part of the body, and in preventing the combustion of Oxygen from doing too much, and preventing the anti-combustion in Nitrogen from doing too much or too little in its office. In this way, by the due presence of these opposite elements in all parts of the Body, and in virtue of the opposing action of each of the other, an atmosphere, if we may so call it, is evolved, in which the Organizing and Perpetuating powers of the Life of Man can exist, and in which they work in harmony with the Sustaining power of Man, on the Line of Principle. The action of the combustion of Oxygen, and the counter influence of an opposite power in Nitrogen, in this case, may be compared in its effect to the action of Mind on the Inertia of Matter, which results in the evolution of Time, in the previous combination of Twenty-four terms, in which life exists.

In this way, the tissues of the Body, in a healthy state, are prevented from being consumed, as in the disease of Consumption, because the anti-combustive property in Nitrogen has lost its power to prevent it, or from perishing from cold, by too much power exerted by the same element.*

The Alimentary System takes similar charge of the food that we receive into the Body, that the Respiratory System does of the air, but the second term, in relation to the first, in Sustaining the Man, acts as a Law to a Principle—one developing the other. It divides the food

---

*The formula may be stated in this way :

1. The Action of Mind.
2. The Inertia of Matter.
3. The Combustion of Oxygen.
4. The Anti-Combustion of Nitrogen.

As is the Action of Mind to the Inertia of Matter, in the evolution of Time, so is the Combustion of Oxygen in the human body to the Anti-Combustion of Nitrogen, as a Condition of the evolution of Mortal Life therein.

But, here are only four terms that, by their opposition, modify each other in action, to the accomplishment of a great purpose, aiming at a constant and essential Use. There must be six of these terms to give order to the unerring progress, and the whole must have similarity in character to enable them to combine. The other two are probably positive and negative Electricity, and the six terms may stand to each other in the following order, from Principal to Use, to-wit :

1. Action of Mind.
2. Inertia of Matter.
3. Positive Electricity.
4. Negative Electricity.
5. Combustion of Oxygen.
6. Anti-Combustion of Nitrogen.

The combination of the formula may be this :

The *Principle* of the Action of Mind, by the *Law* of the Inertia of Matter, flows into Positive Electricity as a *Result:* which Result, by Negative Electricity as a *Cause*, by the Combustion of Oxygen as an *Effect*, flows into Anti-Combustion of Nitrogen as a *Use*.

that we receive into the stomach, and with the organizing and perpetuating powers in Faith, in Time, each particle is separated from other particles, and each and all are weighed and measured, and transported to the place of Use in the formation of new tissue of the Body, and each in its appointed Time, in the order of Principle, Law, Result, Cause and Effect.

The System of the Bones (the Osseous System), is the framework of the Man, and occupies the place of Result. It is the soil in which the Nerves find root, and from which intelligence goes out to move the Muscles, and by which the action of Mind overcomes the Inertia of Matter. In this System the whole Body is *Sustained* in its proper place, and each and every member fixed for its special Use. In the Physical form, it is the *Sustaining Result* of power in Man, and this expression is a type of all its offices in every respect; and all of its offices are represented in the twenty-four vertebrae of the spinal column in Man. If this be firm and strong, all that it upholds will be firm and strong also. On it rests the Mental, Nervous and Muscular Systems of Man. In the sense that the germ of the root sustains the tree, it sustains Human Offspring.

The *Sustaining Cause* of all this action in Man is the Mental System: For, action is a property of Mind, and hence all the movements of Matter in the human Body are caused by the action of Mind overcoming, for specific Use, the Inertia of Matter therein. It affects the Respiratory System as a *Cause* of action in any process affects a *Principle* of action. It affects the Nervous System, as an Effect follows a Cause. Were this System removed from Man, he would be no longer MAN. He would fall, in person and in Species, into the brute or into nothingness.

The *Nervous System* flows from the Mental System as an Effect from a Cause. It is the machinery by which the Mental System conveys its mandates to all parts of the Material Body. By this System, the command is conveyed to the Muscular System, in the attainment of any Use, and it obeys. Mind purposes that the arm be raised. The Nerves convey the command to the appropriate Muscles, and the thing is done. All the other Machinery adapts itself to this specific Use. The action of Mind has overcome the Inertia of Matter, by the direct means of the Nervous and Muscular Systems, and the purpose is accomplished.

The Sixth System is the *Muscular*. It is the *Sustaining* power of action, and its relation to the other five Systems of the Mind, Life and Body is that of USE. All right action terminates in Use. In the Muscles the action of Mind meets the Inertia of Matter, and in them is the battle-field that decides the mastery that fixes the Use. If the purpose of the Mental System, conveyed by the Nerves to the Muscles, cannot by its action overcome the disposition in the Matter of the bone and Muscles to a state of rest, (Inertia,) the arm will not be moved. So of the contrary. All the terms of the Language of Nature are expressed in every right action of the Muscular System. In the combination of the twenty-four terms that flow into the creation of new Offspring, it is the *Sustaining Use*.

The foregoing Systems are the *Sustaining* power of Man in his Personality and hence in his Species.

The Respiratory System has the office of a Sustaining *Principle*.
The Alimentary System has the office of a Sustaining *Law*.
The Osseous System has the office of a Sustaining *Result*.
The Mental System has the office of a Sustaining *Cause*.
The Nervous System has the office of a Sustaining *Effect*.
The Muscular System has the office of a Sustaining *Use*.

The above systems may be read into each other thus, in natural order, in reproduction, to-wit:

The Mental System, as a *Cause* of action, developes the *Principle* of continued life in the Respiratory System, by the *Law* of the Alimentary System, and the Nervous System is the *Effect*. The System of the Bones is the *Result* for the *Use* of the Muscular System.

The fourth family of the twenty-four terms in this combination has the character of *Protection*, in relation to itself and to the three interior families. The terms of the family are these:

1. SELF.
2. NEIGHBOR.
3. SPECIES.
4. MALE.
5. FEMALE.
6. OFFSPRING.

The first of these, Self, as an individual personality, contains the property of Protection in its own right. It can rightfully defend itself from its enemies to the full extent of its power, and this on Principle. We call this Principle the instinct of self-preservation.

This right of Self-protection unites with the like instinct of the Neighbor, which is any other than oneself, as a Principle flows into a Law. The two are then united in Principle and Law. These two terms, *Self* and *Neighbor* include the whole Species of Man. Such is the *Result* of combination for mutual Protection against enemies that are stronger than oneself. Hence, the Principle of Self-protection naturally flows into that of the Protection of the *Species*, as any Principle, by Law, flows into its Result, from Cause and Effect.

The fourth term in this combination is the *Male*, in the two Sexes, in which is contained the Principle and Cause of new life and being in the generation of new Selfhood, to supply the place of those taken away by death.

The fifth term is the *Female*, whose office, in the generation of new Selfhood, for the above purpose, in relation to the Male, is as an Effect to a Cause. The Cause is in the Male, the Effect in the Female.

Offspring, the sixth term, proceeds from the Union of the two sexes, as Male and Female, as Cause and Effect, by Principle and Law, and the Result is a *Protecting Use in Self-preservation of the Species of Man.*

In this combination, Self is the Protecting power on the line of *Principle.*

Neighbor is the Protecting power on the line of *Law.*

Species is the Protecting power on the line of *Result.*

Male is the Protecting power on the line of *Cause.*

Female is the Protecting power on the line of *Effect.*

Offspring is the Protecting power of the Selfhood of the Species on the line of *Use.*

The *Principle* of Protection of human Life in Self, by the *Law* of a similar right in Neighbor, flows into the right of the Protection of the Species of Man as a *Result:* which Result in the Male as a *Cause* by the Female as an *Effect*, flows into Offspring as a *Use.*

These terms, in their order, in reproduction, may be read thus:

The Male, as a *Cause*, developing the *Principle* of new Selfhood in the Neighbor by Marriage, as the *Law*, flows into the Female as an *Effect.* The *Result* is the preservation of the Species of Man in the birth of Offspring, as the great Protecting *Use.*

In the foregoing it will be seen, that the Protecting Uses are these:

1. The Judgment of Mind.
2. The Blood.
3. The Muscular System.
4. Human Offspring.

1. The Judgment of Mind *Organizes*.
2. The Blood *Perpetuates*.
3. The Muscular System *Sustains*.
4. The Offspring Protects the one within the other, all the things of Faith and Time that are represented in the *Offspring* of Man.

The Protecting *Powers* are these:

1. Self.
2. Neighbor.
3. Species.
4. Male.
5. Female.
6. Offspring.

Thus, Offspring is the Great *Protecting Use* that Sustains in continued existence the Species of Man.

OF DIVINE JUSTICE.

We have now completed the fundamental analysis of the three great and comprehensive powers of Faith, Time and Offspring. The fourth power that encompasses the whole is Divine Justice. It is the Protecting power of man in SOCIETY, for in it are represented the Family, the Nation and Providence. It consists of Twenty-four terms, divided into four families, consisting of six members each, to-wit:

1.

1. Father,
2. Mother,
3. Child,
4. Family,
5. Family Government,
6. Family Justice.

2.

1. The Executive Power,
2. The Legislative Power,
3. The Judicial Power,
4. The Popular Power,
5. The National Government,
6. National Justice.

3.

1. The Nervous Temperament,
2. The Bilious Temperament,
3. The Sanguine Temperament,
4. The Lymphatic Temperament,
5. The Providential Government,
6. Providential Justice.

4.

1. God the Father,
2. God the Son,
3. God the Holy Spirit.
4. One God,
5. Divine Government,
6. Divine Justice.

The first of these combinations of power is that of the *Family.* It is the *Organizing* power in Society of Man. If it be full and perfect, all the external powers that *perpetuate, sustain* and *protect* it will be affected in action by it.

The second combination is that of the *Nation.* It envelopes and permeates that of the Family, of which it is the *Perpetuating* power.

The third combination is that of *Providence.* It envelopes and permeates both the Family and the Nation, of whom it is the *Sustaining* power.

The fourth combination is that of the *Divine*. It envelopes and permeates the order and power of the Family, the Nation and of Providence, and is the *Protecting* power of the whole.

The first, in the second, in the third, is protected in the fourth. In this four-fold line of defence is Man and his rights organized, perpetuated, sustained and protected on earth, in Society.

The Effective power in all this is Government, and the Use of *Government* in Society is *Justice*.

Family Justice, in *National Justice*, in *Providential Justice*, finds Protection in *Divine Justice*.

The *Organization* of the Family is *Perpetuated* in the Nation, is *Sustained* in Providence, and *Protected* in the Justice of God.

The Family gives the Nation its *Numbers ;* the Nation gives *Language ;* Providence, in the Temperaments, gives *Power*, and God gives *Creation*.

The Family *Organizes* in Faith ; the Nation *Perpetuates* in Time ; Providence *Sustains* both in Offspring, and all are *Protected* in Divine Justice.

The representative uses of the combination are the four forms of Justice, and the three uses first named and numbered flow into the fourth, which is also the *Protecting* power of the whole.

Let us dwell on the subject of these Governments a little farther. The first is that of the Family, to-wit :

1. FATHER.
2. MOTHER.
3. CHILD.
4. FAMILY.
5. FAMILY GOVERNMENT.
6. FAMILY JUSTICE.

These may be read in the six terms of the Language of Rational Nature as follows, to-wit :

The *Principle* of Life in the Father, by the *Law* of Life in the Mother, flows into the Child in generation as a *Result :* which Result in the Family as a *Cause*, by Family Government as an *Effect*, flows into Family Justice as a *Use*.

The terms that pertain to the National Government are as follows, to-wit:

1. The Executive Power.
2. The Legislative Power.
3. The Judicial Power.
4. The Popular Power.
5. The National Government.
6. National Justice,

which may be read:

The *Principle* of Justice in the Executive power, defined by *Law* in the Legislative power, flows into the Judicial power as a *Result:* which Result in the Popular power as a *Cause*, in National Government as an Effect, flows into the exercise and order of National Justice as a *Use.**

Where these six terms harmonize in action, the Nation fulfils its office, and the People are safe, prosperous and happy. Where there is not harmony of action, and where one usurps the place of another, the disproportion works disorder in the body politic, as it would disease in the individual Man.

The third Habitation and Use of Justice is the Providential. It envelopes National and Family Justice, both of which owe it allegiance, and which it sustains. It exists in the following six ideas or terms:

---

*These terms may be placed in a different form, to more clearly comprehend their relations to each other and to the whole, in reproduction, to-wit:

1. The Executive Power.	*4. The Popular Power.*
2. The Legislative Power.	*5. The National Government.*
3. The Judicial Power.	*6. National Justice.*

The *Popular Power* stands to the *Executive Power* of a Nation as a *Cause* to a *Principle.*

The *Legislative Power* stands to the *National Government* as a *Law* to its *Effect.*

The *Judicial Power* stands to *National Justice* as a *Result* to its *Use.*

In all this—

The *Executive Power* represents *Principle.*

The *Legislative Power* represents *Law.*

The *Judicial Power* represents *Result.*

The *Popular Power* represents *Cause.*

National Government represents *Effect.*

National Justice represents *Use.*

In all reproduction in Nature, a *Cause* of action seeks to develop a *Principle* of action, by appropriate *Law*, for an *Effect*, with a *Result* for a *Use;* so in true Government, the Popular Power, as a *Cause* of action, seeks to develop its *Principle* in the Executive Power, by the Legislative Power in the enactment of appropriate *Laws*, and the whole *Effect* is represented in the Judiciary Power. The *Result* is, National Government, and hence, National Justice as a *Use.*

1. The Nervous Temperament.
2. The Bilious Temperament.
3. The Sanguine Temperament.
4. The Lymphatic Temperament.
5. The Providential Government.
6. Providential Justice.

These Temperaments permeate and encompass all living things, to which they give the power of character in proportion to their fullness in individuals. They bind together all living things, as individuals or nations, internally and externally, as the different systems of power in Man bind together all his parts in one. They are the soil in the being from which actions spring, or by which they govern or obey. God speaks by them to Man, in Man, and by them, in all Nature, he provides man and beast his food, and thus, by general laws, protects all things in life that have life, for their appointed use. By them God raises up leaders to defend the innocent in a righteous cause, and in them the Providence of God can meet the Providence of Man, and govern him for good. It is the third protecting goverment of man, in his personality. In its effect, it gives power to a nation on the general average. In proportion, as the average of the Temperaments of the individuals composing a nation is strong, so will the nation be powerful.

The Fourth and the highest possible Government is the Divine. It exists in the following six terms:

1. God the Father.
2. God the Son.
3. God the Holy Spirit.
4. One God.
5. Divine Government.
6. Divine Justice.

The first three expressions, as related to each other, are one, and cannot be increased or diminished by multiplication or division by or with each other, any more than the number one can be increased by multiplication or division, with or by itself, and as nothing can be subtracted from the selfhood of the Highest Possible, and as nothing can be added to it, the three terms, in relation to each other, are

ONE GOD, and no other form of language can express the meaning.*

Such is the analysis of the four great ideas of Human Progress and Destiny, to-wit:

1. FAITH.
2. TIME.
3. OFFSPRING.
4. DIVINE JUSTICE.

The ninety-six parts, which comprehend the whole, meet in Divine Justice as their sure Protection; and as we can only think of that as a term, in itself as being full and perfect, so we can think of the three terms within it, (Faith, Time and Offspring) as being full and perfect, and this mode of thought will regenerate the world.

If, to the Ninety-six terms, which are contained in Divine Justice, be added the powers of Organization, Perpetuation, Sustenance and Protection, the whole make just one hundred, which number may represent the idea of FULLNESS in Man in completeness. These one hundred terms are so many essential TRUTHS OF GOD, in which the Faith of Man can combine, and in virtue of that combination, there will be a constant approximation to fullness in the generation of Man, in Organization, Perpetuation, Sustenance and Protection, and all the Progress will have been made by a Cause developing a Principle, by its Law, hence an Effect, with a Result, for a Use.

Such is the construction of Man. If it be the true theory when we think of its general plan, we think of man as God thought of him when he created him: and may not that very act of true thought of the mind of man tend to produce the same order in his constant creation now, and consequently tend in a like degree to prevent the disorders that are incident to him in his present state. In other words, the construction of man being in disorder, if we know what his order should be, and if we think of him according to that knowledge, may not the power of that knowledge, or faith, thus exercised in thought, become a positive force to produce order in him, by the Universal Arrangement by which a Principle of Truth flows into a beneficial Use, in the power

---

*In prayer to God, the person praying is in the place of *Cause*, and the Being prayed to in the place of *Principle*. If the *Law* by which the *Cause* developes the *Principle* be complied with in all its appropriate conditions, the *Result* follows in the bestowment of the thing prayed for, the character of the thing prayed for being formed by its intended *Use*.

of God. Think of man as he should be in this depth of his being, and you tend to make him what he should be, for you have in that act of Mind the power of the highest possible government to help you. As you exert the force of your Mind in the right direction, you prevent the formation of the wrong, for truth is always stronger than falsehood, if the two be attended with equal clearness of comprehension and force of character, for it has the help of the Divine Mind. If the knowledge is so clear to the mind as to be received into it as scientific faith, its truth is not then questioned, and it has full and unimpeded power in its action. The love of the good in any person supposes the equal hate of the opposing evil; and by our love and practice of the good, we prevent the evil that otherwise would be.

In Jesus Christ the Language of Universal Power in Creation was fully expressed in every particular and combination, both in the Divine and Human. From his place in the Divine Government he descended by or in the Providential, the National, and the Family Governments into the Human Personal, in which he dwelt in the fullness of Manhood in perfection, subjecting all beneath him to his power, and he became our Law, which place he occupies in the order of the Divine. Thus he opened the way in man from earth to Heaven; and thus, by Christ's virtue, and not by our own, Man may enter into Eternal Life. All that can be expressed in Faith, Time, Offspring and Divine Justice, was and is made perfect in Jesus Christ, and through faith in that power and virtue is to come the "healing of the nations." The Use of Creation was perfected in him, and in the virtue of that perfectness in Humanity comes all true Spirit and Form in Human Progress; for Jesus Christ is an ever living presence. The fulness of power in the Human and Divine is with him to exert for the protection of the Life of man here and hereafter, for in Jesus Christ, in the fullness of DIVINE JUSTICE is the fullness of DIVINE MERCY.

www.ingramcontent.com/pod-product-compliance
Lightning Source LLC
Chambersburg PA
CBHW031756090426
42739CB00008B/1032

* 9 7 8 3 3 3 7 2 3 9 6 2 6 *